Apples for Life

Adán Zepeda

Nancy L Glon

by

Adán Zepeda

illustrations by

Nancy Glon

To school children at
St Louis di Montfort with
appriciation. God bless you!

Nancy Glon,
Illustrator
April 26, 2000

Library of Congress Catalog Card Number 96-92050

ISBN: 0-9651440-0-3

Printed in the United States of America

First Edition

Evangel
Press

2000 Evangel Way
Nappanee, Indiana 46550-0189

This book belongs to~

St. Louis de Montfort

Catholic School

Library

Our thanks and gratitude to those who have
helped to make this book come from a
dream to a reality, and especially to
Leo Pineda for his knowledge and
invaluable information.

This book is dedicated to the Zepeda and
Glon families and to all children of all ages
everywhere who love to learn.

Morning Dew

The morning was wet
with one hundred percent humidity~
my old bones hurt
hoping the sun would appear.

For the intensity of the fog
it was hard to see the apples;
the stiff joints in my body
hurt climbing up the ladder.

My shoes were soaking wet~
the canvas bag felt like a rock.
Voices in the dark ask me,
"Do you see the apples?"

"No, not yet; it's too early."
"Did you wash your face this morning?"
"Oh, yeah, I always do...
with the morning dew."

Adán Zepeda

Here are two men planting apple
trees. The planting is done in March
or April when it is a little chilly in
northern Indiana.

These little trees are just a few
months old when they are brought
from the apple nursery. They are from
thirty to forty inches tall and have
small roots and almost no branches.

After several weeks in the ground, some apple growers paint the little trees white about thirty inches from the ground. Why? The paint protects the trees from rabbits and other animals that hunt for food during the winter.

Another way to protect the little trees
is to put a fragrant bar of soap on
every tree; deer like to eat young
apple trees. The smell of the soap
makes them believe a human is close
by so they won't go near it giving the
trees time to grow instead.

The next year some apple growers put clothes pins on their branches. Why, you wonder. The clothes pins cause the branches to spread out and make nicely shaped trees. The trees will need to be pruned every year to keep their shape.

8

If the trees are well cared for, they will have beautiful flowers. One little flower makes a big juicy apple. However, hard rains and strong winds may knock some flowers off and then there are fewer apples.

9

These four year old apple trees have hundreds and hundreds of flowers. Unfortunately this is also a dangerous time of year. Sometimes a cold front whips the region with freezing temperatures and the apple growers lose their crop.

Have you noticed those wooden boxes in the orchards? Inside there are thousands of honey bees. Their job is to pollinate the flowers of every tree. They fly from flower to flower to get the sweet nectar to make honey, the kind you see in jars in the supermarkets.

The pollen from the blossoms collects on the legs of the bees as they fly from flower to flower. The pollen is passed from flower to flower, too. After a few weeks, the petals fall and soon you begin to see the little green apples. They are very sour and will need time to grow and ripen to develop their sweetness.

If conditions are better than usual, too many apples may begin to grow. When this happens, the growers might thin them. This is done by using a chemical spray which causes some of the marble-sized apples to drop off. Thinning can also be done by hand but takes much longer.

The weather is an important factor and a major concern of the apple growers. For example, what you see here are huge wind machines with big propellers. The propellers are turned by a powerful diesel engine on the side of the machine; they push the warm air from above down through the trees below when the temperature drops to the freezing point, 32°F. The warm air keeps the tiny apples warm, too.

A costly way to save the apples is to hire a helicopter and pilot to help. The helicopter flies back and forth over the coldest spots. The air is warmer forty to fifty feet off the ground and the motion of the blades of the helicopter forces the warm air down. Knowing where the coldest spots are is important for the pilot. And it is really a very simple matter to let him know.

120
110
100
90
80
70
60
50
40
30
20
10
0
10
20
30

FAHRENHEIT TEMP

One or two men work during the night checking the thermometers they have in the orchards. When they find a cold spot, they signal the helicopter pilot with their flashlight to fly over until the temperature rises in that particular area.

Some other apple growers use oil
heater devices trying to save their
crop. Someone has to be in charge of
putting the oil in the heaters and
firing them up to heat the coldest
spots in the freezing temperatures.

When the apples are fully grown, they have beautiful color and a very, very wonderful taste. But too many apples are not good for the tree, especially on young trees. The weight of the apples sometimes breaks the branches because the branches are too thin.

The older trees are stronger; they can hold the weight of hundreds and hundreds of apples. Unfortunately, when the trees grow too tall, some apple growers have to trim them down to be able to reach the fruit from their tops. They also trim them on their sides which makes the trees look as if they are square.

But how do they do that? Some `growers
have a machine like this one you see here.
This machine costs thousands of dollars
but does the job well. It can cut branches
up to three or four inches in diameter.

The apple pickers prefer the young trees more than the old trees. They are not as tall and the apples are easier to pick. Since the pickers pick by the bushel, they can make more money. Not just anybody can pick apples. It takes skill and much experience to be a fast and good picker.

The apples are very delicate and can be bruised easily. That is why the apple pickers use special canvas bags to protect the fruit. They also must carry a sixteen foot ladder to get the fruit from the tops of the trees. A good apple picker can pick up to two hundred bushels a day if the crop is good.

Some apple growers have warehouses like giant refrigerators where hundreds of bushels of apples are stored. Others have special rooms with controlled atmospheres that can keep the apples fresh and crisp for six months or longer—as long as the room remains unopened.

The apples are taken from the storage building to the
local supermarkets and out of state in big trucks. The
trucks have refrigeration units to keep the apples cool
until they get to their final destination.

If you have ever wondered where the cider comes from, here is how it is done. This special machine cuts the apples in small pieces and presses them between the rollers. The apple juice then drops into the tank. The apple skins and seeds run out on a conveyor belt to be transported to the fields and returned to the soil.

CIDER

100% Pure Apples

1995

After they press hundreds of bushels of apples, the apple grower stores the cider in big stainless steel tanks. Later, it will be put into gallon and half gallon containers. The delicious taste is achieved by pressing several kinds of apples which gives much better flavor.

You might be surprised to learn how many apples are needed to make one gallon of cider. It depends on the size and variety of apples.

Usually, one bushel of big apples makes approximately three to three and a half gallons of cider. One bushel of apples can weigh as much as forty-two pounds.

25

There are fifty-six jumbo sized apples in one bushel, but it also takes one hundred thirty-eight of the smaller apples to fill a bushel. In supermarkets and fruit stands you will find apples of all sizes, varieties and colors.

Another fact for you to know and remember is how long
an apple tree can live and produce apples. It depends on
the earth where it is planted, the weather, and the kind of
care it receives as the tree grows. This golden delicious
apple tree is approximately seventy-five to eighty years
old and is still producing many, many tasty apples.

Apple growers are constantly growing new and better varieties of apples. For example, these four year old trees used to be a particular variety of apple. For one reason or another, the grower did not like it—maybe it was too small or too tart—so someone was sent to cut most of the branches off and a new and better variety was grafted onto the old trunk.

28

Here, only two years later, you can see the same apple tree loaded with golden delicious apples; and they are very, very delicious—I recommend them. Now you know how the apple growers grow the apple trees to get all those apples. You have read the book and looked at the pictures.

The apple grower always tries to produce apples in ways that can be least costly to them and also to the consumer— that's YOU! To help you save money sometimes you may be allowed to pick your own apples. Perhaps you have seen signs that read "YOU PICK" in front of the orchards.

The latest way to grow apples is shown here: apple trees that grow almost like vines, close together and very dense. The limbs are encouraged to grow along wire supports. They are easier to prune, spray and harvest and they get more sun helping the apple to grow more red in color. There are many more trees per acre which means more apples for everyone.

This is only part of the apple's story. There are many
more ways to use the apple: apple butter, apple pie,
apple dumplings, apple juice, carmel apples, applesauce
and just a plain apple. Some people even carve apples,
let them dry and then make dolls. You can probably
think of many more ways to use the delicious apple.

Some gifts of the apple tree...

APPLE TREES

*The apple trees are resting
after their fruit is gone,
the leaves fly with the wind
and that is not a pretty tone.*

*The winter is cold indeed
the coming crop is unknown,
the apples run cross country
like the biggest marathon.*

A.Z.

THE AUTHOR

Adán Zepeda was born in Ricardo, Texas, in 1935, eventually moving to Goshen, Indiana, in 1973. It was while he was driving a delivery truck, that he began writing poetry and some short stories. As his English improved, he was able to write in his new language as well as Spanish even though he was unable to attend any formal educational classes. One day, while working at the Kercher Orchards, he was struck with the idea to write a book about the apple tree and the process involved in growing and producing apples. The idea included helping the St. John Evangelist Catholic School in Goshen. The finished book was a four and a half year project. Mr. Zepeda is currently working on several stories and a novel and has already published a book of poems entitled "Lagrimas Y Sonrisas" (Laughter and Tears). He is the father of six and lives in Goshen with his wife, Herlinda.

THE ILLUSTRATOR

Even as a mother of seven, Nancy Glon has always found time to write, draw, paint, design cards, teach calligraphy and address wedding invitations and do anything in the world of creativity. She has been in business with her husband, John, and in the field of education off and on for over forty years. But she has always had a little dream of her own. That was to publish a book. When she and Mr. Zepeda met at St. John's, the dream took flight and has now become a reality. Surprise still lights up her face when people refer to her as an artist. The Glon's moved to Goshen, Indiana, in 1994, where they enjoy the "good life."

Underwriters

Jacquelynn Mills
Elizabeth Rieth

Donors

Kercher Sunrise Orchards, Inc.
19498 County Road 38
Goshen, Indiana 46526
(219) 533-6317

Mi Casita Restaurant
Authentic Mexican Food
2124 Elkhart Road
Goshen, Indiana 46526

Mrs. Charles Lanham

Mr. and Mrs. H. Dale Showalter